W9-AFU-634

Patterson Elementary School
3731 Lawrence Drive
Naperville, IL 60564

AaBbCcDdEeFfGgHh

The ABCs of
Habitats

Bobbie Kalman

🌳 Crabtree Publishing Company

www.crabtreebooks.com

A a B b C c D d E e F f G g H h

The ABCs of the Natural World

Created by Bobbie Kalman

Dedicated by Robin Johnson
For Mom and Dad, with love sweet love

Author and Editor-in-Chief
Bobbie Kalman

Editors
Reagan Miller
Robin Johnson

Photo research
Crystal Sikkens

Design
Bobbie Kalman
Katherine Kantor
Samantha Crabtree (cover)

Production coordinator
Katherine Kantor

Illustrations
Barbara Bedell: pages 6, 9, 10, 20, 23, 26 (sea shore), 30 (frog)
Katherine Kantor: pages 8 (blue tang and masked rabbitfish), 13,
     17, 26 (limpet and crab), 28 (dirt), 30 (cattails)
Cori Marvin: page 8 (lionfish)
Jeannette McNaughton-Julich: page 8 (dolphin)
Bonna Rouse: pages 8 (sea turtle and sea star), 26 (bird)
Margaret Amy Salter: pages 21, 24

Photographs
© iStockphoto.com: pages 13 (bottom), 22 (tadpole), 24 (top left),
     25 (top left), 26 (sea urchins and clam), 29 (top), 30
© 2008 Jupiterimages Corporation: back cover
© Shutterstock.com: pages 1 (bottom), 3, 4, 5 (bottom left and right),
     6, 7, 8 (bottom), 9, 10, 11, 12, 13 (top), 14 (bottom), 16 (left), 17,
     19 (top), 21, 22 (except tadpole), 23 (bottom), 24 (butterflies),
     25 (bottom right), 26 (nautilus and sea star), 27, 28, 31
Other images by Adobe Image Library, Corbis, Corel, Creatas,
     Digital Stock, Digital Vision, Eyewire, and Photodisc

Library and Archives Canada Cataloguing in Publication

Kalman, Bobbie, 1947-
     The ABCs of habitats / Bobbie Kalman.

(The ABCs of the natural world)
Includes index.
ISBN 978-0-7787-3411-6 (bound)
ISBN 978-0-7787-3431-4 (pbk.)

     1. Habitat (Ecology)--Juvenile literature. 2. Biotic communities--Juvenile
literature. 3. English language--Alphabet--Juvenile literature. I. Title.
II. Series: ABCs of the natural world

QL756.K34 2007   j577   C2007-904240-6

Library of Congress Cataloging-in-Publication Data

Kalman, Bobbie.
     The ABCs of habitats / Bobbie Kalman.
          p. cm. -- (The ABCs of the natural world)
     Includes index.
     ISBN-13: 978-0-7787-3411-6 (rlb)
     ISBN-10: 0-7787-3411-0 (rlb)
     ISBN-13: 978-0-7787-3431-4 (pb)
     ISBN-10: 0-7787-3431-5 (pb)
     1. Animals--Habitations--Juvenile literature. 2. English language--
Alphabet--Juvenile literature. I. Title. II. Series.

QL756.K35 2007
577--dc22

                                   2007026976

Crabtree Publishing Company

www.crabtreebooks.com   1-800-387-7650

Copyright © **2008 CRABTREE PUBLISHING COMPANY**. All rights reserved. No part of this publication may be reproduced, stored in a
retrieval system or be transmitted in any form or by any means, electronic, mechanical, photocopying, recording, or otherwise, without the prior
written permission of Crabtree Publishing Company. In Canada: We acknowledge the financial support of the Government of Canada through the
Book Publishing Industry Development Program (BPIDP) for our publishing activities.

Published in Canada
Crabtree Publishing
616 Welland Ave.
St. Catharines, Ontario
L2M 5V6

Published in the United States
Crabtree Publishing
PMB16A
350 Fifth Ave., Suite 3308
New York, NY 10118

Published in the United Kingdom
Crabtree Publishing
White Cross Mills
High Town, Lancaster
LA1 4XS

Published in Australia
Crabtree Publishing
386 Mt. Alexander Rd.
Ascot Vale (Melbourne)
VIC 3032

Contents

Animals adapt

green anole

Animals live all over Earth. There are animals living in very hot places and in very cold places. The natural places where plants and animals live are called **habitats**. Animals **adapt**, or become suited, to the habitats in which they live. Not all animals can live in every kind of habitat.

The green anole above lives in a hot rain forest. This polar bear could not live in a rain forest. It has a fur coat, and it would feel too hot. The polar bear's habitat is very cold for most of the year.

Mountain goats live in mountain habitats.

Martens live in a forest habitat.

Leopards live in a grassland habitat.

Desert tortoises live in desert habitats.

Dolphins live in ocean habitats.

Frogs live in pond habitats.

5

Backyard habitats

ladybird beetle

Many animals live in backyard habitats. Some of their names start with the letter B. Birds, butterflies, bees, and bugs of all kinds live in back yards. Ladybird beetles also live in back yards.

Blue jays visit backyard bird feeders in winter. It is hard to find food in winter.

Some animals visit back yards to find food. Which of these animals visit back yards? Which animal does not visit? Do bunnies visit back yards? Do squirrels visit back yards? Do chipmunks visit back yards? Do bears visit back yards? Have you ever seen one in yours?

Bunnies visit back yards.

This baby squirrel is visiting a back yard.

Do chipmunks visit back yards?

Are there bears in your back yard?

7

Colorful coral reefs

Coral polyps look like flowers, but they are animals.

Coral reefs are warm, shallow ocean habitats, that contain colorful **corals**. Corals are made up of tiny animals called **coral polyps**. Many kinds of fish and other animals live in coral reefs. Sea turtles and dolphins also spend time in coral reefs.

dolphin

sea turtle

blue tang   masked rabbitfish   lionfish   sea star

Dd Dd Dd Dd Dd Dd Dd Dd

Dry deserts

Deserts are dry habitats that get very little rain. There are hot deserts and cold deserts. The desert shown here is the Sinai Desert in Africa. This desert is very hot and dry, but some palms are growing in this spot. There must be water below the ground! An area in a dry desert where plants grow is called an **oasis**.

Camels live in deserts. They do not need to drink water every day.

Palms are plants. They look like trees, but they have no branches. Trees have branches.

Endangered!

There are **endangered** animals in almost every habitat. Endangered animals are in danger of disappearing from Earth forever. Rhinoceroses, or rhinos, are endangered. They are losing their habitats to people. Rhino habitats include forests, mountains, and grassy areas. People use the land in these habitats for farming. Rhinos then have no place to live. The rhinos above are Asian rhinos. There are fewer than 2,500 Asian rhinoceroses left in the world.

Forest habitats

Ff Ff Ff Ff Ff Ff Ff Ff Ff Ff Ff Ff Ff

Forests are areas of land covered with trees. There are many kinds of forests. **Boreal forests** grow in places with cold winters. Boreal forests are also called **coniferous forests**. **Conifers** grow in these forests. Conifers are trees with cones. The leaves of conifers are thin and sharp like needles.

cone

Many kinds of owls live in coniferous forests. These owls are great horned owls.

Grasslands

Grasslands are huge areas where grasses and a few trees grow. Grasslands grow all over the world. They have different names. In North America, grasslands are called **plains** or **prairies**. In South America, they are called **pampas**. Animals called guanacos live on the pampas. Guanaco starts with the letter G.

These guanacos are eating grasses on grasslands called pampas. These grasslands can be found in the countries of Chile and Argentina. Both countries are in South America.

G g G g G g G g G   G g G g

Some grasslands in Africa are called **savannas**. The weather in savannas is hot and can be very dry. Small trees and bushes grow on these grasslands, and many animals live there. Zebras, elephants, cheetahs, and giraffes are just a few of these animals. Which animal's name starts with G?

giraffe

elephant

zebras

This cheetah is looking for animals to hunt on the savanna.

Hh Hh Hh Hh Hh Hh Hh

Human habitats

Some people live in towns.
Towns are smaller than cities.

Human beings are people. People live in homes. Their homes are in human habitats such as cities, towns, and **villages**. Villages are small towns. Cities, towns, and villages can be found in deserts and near grasslands. Human habitats are also near forests, wetlands, and oceans. People live almost everywhere.

This city is Vancouver, Canada. It is near mountains and beside the Pacific Ocean.
There are also forests near Vancouver. Many animals live in the natural habitats near this city.

14

Icy habitats

I i I i I i I i I i I i I i I i I i I i

Polar bears live in the Arctic. The Arctic is a cold habitat near the North Pole. Ice and snow cover much of the Arctic. In summer, plants grow on the land, which is called the **tundra** (see page 27). Antarctica is another cold habitat. It also has a lot of ice and snow. Antarctica is near the South Pole. The penguins shown right live in Antarctica.

Jungles are hot!

Jungles are like rain forests (see page 24). Jungles have many trees, bushes, and other plants. The plants grow closely together. Jungles are found in Southeast Asia and in Africa. In jungles, there is a rainy season. During the rainy season, heavy rainfall soaks the forests. The rain helps the many plants grow. The tiger and orangutan below both live in a jungle. The jungle is on an island called Sumatra in Southeast Asia.

16

Kk Kk Kk Kk Kk Kk Kk Kk Kk Kk

Kelp forests

Unlike other forests, **kelp forests** do not grow on land. They grow in shallow ocean waters. **Kelp** is not a plant. It is the largest type of **alga**. Alga is like a plant, but it has no roots, stems, or leaves.

Seaweed is alga, and kelp is the largest type of seaweed. Kelp can grow as tall as 160 feet or 50 meters. Many animals live in kelp forests. Sea otters wrap themselves in kelp before going to sleep so they will not drift away.

Kelp forests look like underwater jungles.

17

Lakes and land

Lakes are big bodies of water with land around them. Lakes can be large, but they are not as large as oceans. The water in lakes is **fresh water**. Fresh water is not salty like the water in oceans. Many kinds of fish live in lakes. Birds such as swans find food in lakes. Moose find grasses and other plants to eat on the shores of lakes.

There are thousands of lakes on Earth! Is there a lake near where you live?

M m M m M m M m M m M m
Mountain habitats

Mountains are tall, steep areas of land. Some mountains are covered with grasses. Other mountains are rocky. The weather is cold at the tops of high mountains. Forests grow at the bottom of most mountains. Some forests grow on mountains, too. Mountain gorillas live in cool, misty forests that are high up on mountains. These mountains are in the central part of Africa.

Wild horses feed on the grasses on a mountaintop.

Mountain gorillas live in groups with family members. How many gorillas are in this group?

N n N n N n N n N n N n N n N n

National parks

National parks are huge safe habitats for wildlife. People are not allowed to hunt or build in these parks. National parks are run by the governments of countries. Yellowstone National Park was the very first national park in the world. It is home to animals such as wolves, grizzly bears, elk, and bison. Today, there are national parks in many countries around the world.

Wolves are protected in national parks such as Yellowstone National Park in the United States and Banff National Park in Canada.

Ocean habitats

Oceans are large water habitats. They are made up of salt water. There are warm oceans and cold oceans. Cold oceans are covered with ice and snow. Oceans are full of wonderful animals. Which ocean animal names start with O? They are octopus and orca! Orcas are large dolphins. They are also called killer whales. The orca in the picture above is **breaching**. Breaching is leaping high out of water.

An octopus is an ocean animal with a big head and eight arms.

Pond life

A **pond** is a small lake with fresh water. Many animals live in ponds. Fish, such as the red koi on the left, live in ponds. Birds and many other animals find food in ponds. Frogs lay eggs called **spawn** in ponds. The eggs hatch into many tadpoles. The tadpoles soon become frogs.

frog spawn   *tadpole*

Quiz about habitats

Do this quiz after you have read the whole book. You can find the answers on the pages listed beside each question.

1. Which animals make up coral reefs? Name four animals that live in coral reefs. (page 8)
2. Which habitat has trees with cones? What are the trees called? Which bird lives in this habitat? (page 11)
3. Guanaco starts with G. What is its habitat? It has two names. One starts with G, and the other with P. (page 12)
4. Which kind of forest grows in the ocean? (page 17)
5. What do some horses and gorillas have in common? (see page 19)
6. What is the name of the first national park? (page 20)
7. Which two ocean animals' names start with the letter O? (page 21)
8. Name a famous wetland in Florida. (page 30)

What are these called? (page 8)

Where does this owl live?

What is this animal called?

RrRrRrRrRrRrRrRrR

Rainy rain forests

Habitats get different amounts of rain. Rain forests get a lot of rain all year. Many plants grow in rain forests because there is plenty of water. Rain forests also have many kinds of animals. Some are tiny, such as butterflies and ants. Others are large, like the cougar shown below. Rain forests that are hot all year are called **tropical rain forests**. Tropical rain forests get rain nearly every day!

Cougars live in many habitats. This cougar lives in a rain forest in South America.

R r R r R r R r R r R r R r R r

Three-toed sloths live in tropical rain forests.

Tree frogs also live in tropical rain forests.

Rain forests that are cool and wet are called **temperate rain forests**. Temperate rain forests are in areas of the world that have cold winters and warm summers. In winter, there is not much food for animals to eat. There is plenty of food in spring and summer. This elk is eating the new plants that are growing in spring.

Seashores

limpet

clam

*sea urchin
out of shell*

*sea urchin
inside shell*

Seashores are places where oceans meet land. Some seashores are rocky, and others are sandy. Each day, the water falls at **low tide** and rises at **high tide**. At high tide, many sea animals are washed up on the shores. At low tide, the water moves away from the shores. Some water is trapped between the rocks, forming **tide pools**. Animals such as sea stars, sea urchins, crabs, shrimps, and mollusks are also trapped in the tide pools.

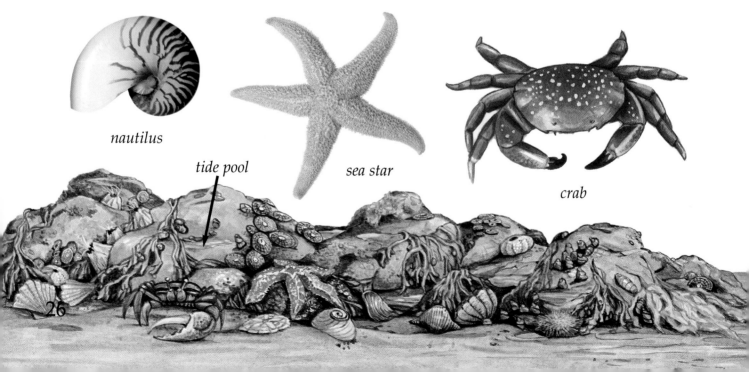

nautilus

tide pool

sea star

crab

26

Tt Tt Tt Tt Tt Tt Tt Tt Tt Tt
Treeless tundras

Tundras are cold deserts. These habitats are in cold, windy areas. Only certain kinds of plants can grow on tundras because much of the ground is frozen. Ground that stays frozen all year is called **permafrost**. Trees cannot grow in permafrost. Plants on the tundra grow close to the ground because strong winds blow away tall plants.

More than 400 kinds of flowers grow on tundras!

The plants that grow on tundras turn colors in the fall, just as the leaves of some trees do. This deer finds food on the tundra.

27

Underground homes

Some animals live in underground habitats. Living under the ground keeps these animals safe from **predators**. Predators are animals that hunt and eat other animals. Groundhogs, armadillos, prairie dogs, and earthworms live under the ground, but all these animals spend time above ground, too.

*This baby groundhog is peeking out of its underground tunnel home, called a **burrow**.*

28

Vanishing habitats

Vanishing means disappearing. Many habitats on Earth are getting smaller. Some are gone forever. People are using land for farming or for building. Large areas of rain forests are being cut down or burned to build farms. The animals that lived in these forests have lost their homes. Without homes, many of these animals die.

These pictures show rain forests being cut down or burned. Where can the animals go?

Wetland habitats

Wetlands are areas of land that are covered with water for at least part of the year. There are many plants and animals living in and around wetland habitats. Alligators live in wetlands, and many birds visit wetlands to rest and to find food. People also visit wetlands to enjoy activities such as hiking, canoeing, and camping. The wetland above is part of the Everglades in Florida.

EXplore!

The Earth is an **eXtremely** beautiful planet. It is a planet with **eXtra**-special places to **eXplore**. It is full of **eXciting** animals and **eXotic** plants. **You** can learn more about the Earth by taking walks in nature, by watching nature shows, or by reading books. Do not forget to visit the zoo near you, too!

You at the Zoo

These kids are watching a bear at a zoo.

Some zoos look like the natural habitats of animals. Animals have trees to climb and room to roam around. These zoos often help animals by teaching people about them. Find out what the zoo near you does to help animals.

AaBbCcDdEeFfGgHh

Glossary

Note: Some boldfaced words are defined where they appear in the book.

breaching Rising high above water

coniferous forest A forest in which trees with cones, called conifers, grow

coral polyp A tiny ocean animal that has no brain or backbone and cannot move from place to place

fresh water Water that does not contain a lot of salt, as ocean water does

jungle A dense forest that gets a lot of rain during parts of the year

oasis A spot in a desert where water is found and where plants grow

permafrost A thick layer of soil that stays frozen the whole year

savanna A grassy plain with a few trees that is found in hot, dry places

spawn A clump of many eggs laid by fish, frogs, and other animals

temperate rain forest A rain forest in an area with mostly mild weather

tropical rain forest A rain forest located in an area that has hot weather year round

Index

Printed in the U.S.A.